Sweets for a Treat

by Gwenda Parker

Photographs by Fiona Parker

Coconut ice is an easy sweet to make for a treat. It looks nice and tastes even better. Serve some at a party. Give some away for a gift or make some to sell.

To make coconut ice you will need:

- 1 tablespoon of butter
- 2 cups of sugar
- 150 mls ($^2/3$ cup) of milk
- salt
- one small cup of coconut
- food colouring

You will also need:

- a big pot
- a stirring spoon
- a greased flat dish
- a beater
- a bowl

Melt the butter in a big pot.
Add the sugar, then the milk and a pinch of salt.
Turn the heat to medium.
Bring the mixture to the boil.
Stir, then boil gently for ten minutes.

Take the pot off the heat.
Add the coconut.
Stir to mix.
Put half the mixture into the bowl.
Beat this mixture until it's thick.
Pour it into the greased dish.

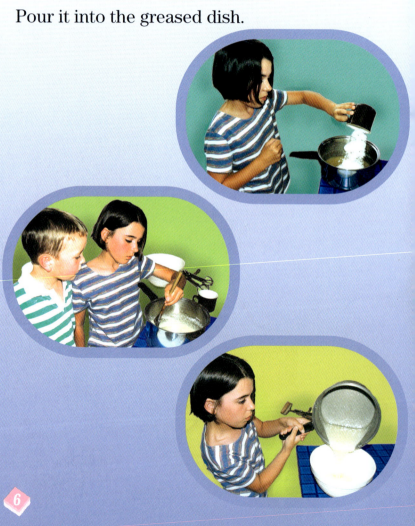

Add a few drops of food colouring to the mixture in the pot.
Beat this mixture until it's thick.
Pour the coloured mixture on top of the white mixture in the dish.
Let the coconut ice set and cool. Cut it into squares.

To give away as a gift or to sell, put the pieces of coconut ice in a clear bag.
Tie the top with a coloured ribbon.

Coconut ice - sweets for a treat.